■
Black Box

REVIEW COPY

Please email reviews

and comments to:

poetry@coppercanyonpress.org

Books by Erin Belieu

Black Box

The Extraordinary Tide:
New Poetry by American Women, co-editor

One Above & One Below

Infanta

black box

erin belieu

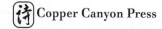Copper Canyon Press

Cover art: *Wet*, 6.25" × 6.25", oil and acrylic on paper, copyright 2002 by Brenda Chrystie / CORBIS

Copper Canyon Press is in residence at Fort Worden State Park in Port Townsend, Washington, under the auspices of Centrum Foundation. Centrum is a gathering place for artists and creative thinkers from around the world, students of all ages and backgrounds, and audiences seeking extraordinary cultural enrichment.

LIBRARY OF CONGRESS CATALOGING-IN-PUBLICATION DATA

Belieu, Erin
Black box: poems / by Erin Belieu.
    p.   cm.
ISBN 1-55659-251-5 (pbk.: alk. paper)
I. Title.
PS3552.E479B57 2006
811'.54—dc22

                                                    2006014357

9 8 7 6 5 4 3 2 FIRST PRINTING

COPPER CANYON PRESS
Post Office Box 271
Port Townsend, Washington 98368
www.coppercanyonpress.org

■

This book is dedicated to Allison Jenks
and Tom Jungerberg

Acknowledgment goes to the magazines in which many of these poems first appeared (sometimes in slightly different versions):

Barrow Street

Can We Have Our Ball Back

Columbia: A Journal of Literature and Art

Electronic Poetry Review

Ploughshares

Tin House

TriQuarterly

The Virginia Quarterly Review

I would also like to thank the friends who helped in the process of writing this book: Susan Aizenberg, Julianna Baggott, Josh Bell, Mark Bibbins, Adam Boles, Cynie Cory, Cameron Diskin, Andrew Epstein, Martín Espada, Ted Genoways, Sam Hamill, Scott Hightower, Kay Auxier Horwath, Chris Jones, Kai Lashley, Rosie Ledbetter, Eric Lee, Richard Osborne, Carl Phillips, Andrew Sneddon, Joe Stroud, and Mark Wunderlich.

—Ungenerous!—to seize upon the wreck of an unwary passenger, whom your subjects had beckon'd to their coast—by heaven! SIRE, it is not well done; and much does it grieve me, 'tis the monarch of a people so civilized and courteous, and so renown'd for sentiment and fine feelings, that I have to reason with——

But I have scarce set foot in your dominions——

LAURENCE STERNE,
A Sentimental Journey through France and Italy

Contents

Black Box

Of the Poet's Youth

When the man behind the counter said, "You pay
by the orifice," what could we do but purchase them all?

Ah, Sandy, you were clearly the deluxe doll, modish and pert
in your plastic nurse whites, official hostess to our halcyon days,

where you bobbed in the doorway of our dishabille apartment,
a block downwind from the stockyards. Holding court on

the corroded balcony, K. and I passed hash brownies, collecting
change for the building's monthly pool to predict which balcony

would fall off next. That's when K. was fucking M. and M. was
fucking J., and even B. and I threw down once on the glass-speckled

lawn, adrift in the headlights of his El Camino. Those were immortal
times, Sandy! Coke wasn't addictive yet, condoms prevented herpes

and men were only a form of practice for the Russian novel
we foolishly hoped our lives would become. Now it's a Friday night,

sixteen years from there. Don't the best characters know better
than to live too long? My estranged husband house-sits for a spoiled

cockatoo while saving to buy his own place. My lover's gone back
to his gin and the farm-team fiancée he keeps in New York.

What else to do but read Frank O'Hara to my tired three-year-old?
When I put him to bed, he mutters "more sorry" as he turns into sleep.

Tonight, I find you in a box I once marked "The Past." Well,
therapy's good for some things, Sandy, but who'd want to forgive

a girl like that? Frank says *Destroy yourself if you don't know!*
Deflated, you're simply the smile that surrounds a hole.
                                        I don't know anything.

i

Epithalamion

the creature of our most commodious sacrament...

Comes gooseberry yenta,
goblin of misalignment.

Comes a black charm, baked, ribbon
and all, into the virgin cake.

Comes aboriginal into the silks and
sweat-fumed underthings.

Comes penny-headed.

Comes a fiend waxing blisters
into the lucky foot.

Comes fishwife of tantrum and crooked
silence, Plantagenet despot wasting his reign.

Comes ulcerous
and dangerous in person.

Comes strangely beguiled, humble
uncorked ideal.

Comes the upended bucket, chrome
trophy hiding its galaxy of holes.

Comes ambivalent as the sheet
you hang botched,

the glyph rampant
heralding our bloody news.

The Birthmark

for Jude

You showed up late and angry.
You shat upon the floor.

With that, how could we fail
to recognize you: Your father,

grief's tent-show wizard,
the long connected silks pouring
from his sleeve. And your mother?

Haven't you known me wholly
as the spider knows each tilting
and imperfect room she sews
to be uncertain ground?

Everyone was out to get you —

The world jabbed you
with its needle, smeared its burning
ointment in your eyes.
Half-garroted by your cord,

you were the cartoon man
who leaps from one inferno
to land with blistered feet inside
another. Those first months were

cold as an apology. The dogwood
outside your bedroom tapped at
the windows, freezing in her gown
of clouded ice. You won't remember this:

the terms of our arrangement,
the shotgun service our bodies planned
without ceremony or consent.

Once upon a time...
you broke free from me, mad
with mourning, but now you're
a different soul. When did you begin
to laugh just to listen to your own

instrument? When did every snakebit
stray in the neighborhood start
to limp behind you, as if joy
were contagious and you its fever? Now

even your father smiles, confused when
he forgets not to. Last night I rocked you
when you refused to sleep, your lips parted

on my cheek, your wet exhalations no
bigger than a runt's. Drifting off
you took my finger in your hand,
pulled it to your mouth, and bit me.

Today I find a sore, unfinished moon
where you've fixed it, beneath my nail.

Last Trip to the Island

You're mad that I can't love the ocean,

but I've come to this world landlocked
and some bodies feel permanently strange.
Like any foreign language, study it too late and
it never sticks. Anyway,

we're here aren't we? —
trudging up the sand, the water churning
its constant horny noise, an openmouthed heavy

breathing made more unnerving by
the presence of all these families, the toddlers

with their chapped bottoms, the fathers
in gigantic trunks spreading out their dopey
circus-colored gear.

How can anyone relax
near something so worked up all the time?

I know the ocean is glamorous,
but the hypnosis, the dilated pull of it, feels

impossible to resist. And what better reason to
resist? I'm most comfortable in

a field, a yellow-eared patch
of cereal, whose quiet rustling argues for
the underrated valor of discretion.

And above this, I admire a certain quality of
sky, like an older woman who wears her jewels with
an air of distance, that is, lightly,
with the right attitude. Unlike your ocean,

there's nothing sneaky about a field. I like their
ugly-girl frankness. I like that, sitting in the dirt,

I can hear what's coming between the stalks.

After Reading That the Milky Way
Is Devouring the Galaxy of Sagittarius

at the Dorothy B. Oven Park

I'm certain Mrs. Oven
meant to be nice
when she bequeathed that everything
in her garden should be nice
forever. This explains

one version of paradise:
the tiny gazebo with fluted
piecrust for a roof, the footbridge
spanning a tinkly stream
small enough to step over.
Even this snail drags

an iridescent skid mark
around the fountain's marble
lip. His shell is an enormous
earring like the ones my mother
wore to prom in 1957,
that large, that optimistic.
And because we're never alone
in paradise, my son is here.

He's stolen a silver balloon from
the wedding party posing for
photos before a copse of live oaks,
the trees shawled in moss like
hand-tatted mantillas. Secretly,

I applaud his thievery. And
the bride as well, looking five months
gone, I guess, wearing Mouseketeer
ears with her stupendous gown.
Good for her. Best to keep

two hands on your sense of humor.
Best to ignore those other worlds
exploding, how violently, how
quietly, they come and go.

for Andrew Epstein

I Heart Your Dog's Head

I'm watching football, which is odd as
I hate football
in a hyperbolic and clinically revealing way,
but I hate Bill Parcells more,
because he is the illuminated manuscript
of cruel, successful men, those with the slitty eyes of ancient reptiles,
who wear their smugness like a tight white turtleneck,
and revel in their lack of empathy
for any living thing.
So I'm watching football, staying up late to watch football,
hoping to witness (as I think of it)
The Humiliation of the Tuna
(as he is called),
which is rightly Parcells's first time back in the Meadowlands
since taking up with the Cowboys,
who are, as we all know,
thugs, even by the NFL's standards. The reasons

I hate football are clear and complicated and were born,
as I was, in Nebraska,
where football is to life what sleep deprivation is
to Amnesty International, that is,
the best researched and most effective method
of breaking a soul. Yes,

there's the glorification of violence, the weird nexus
knitting the homo, both phobic and erotic,
but also, and worse, my parents in 1971, drunk as
Australian parrots in a bottlebush, screeching
WE'RE #1, WE'RE #1!
when the Huskers finally clinched the Orange Bowl,
the two of them
bouncing up and down crazily on the couch, their index
fingers jutting holes through the ubiquitous trail of smoke rings
that was the weather in our house,
until the whole deranged mess that was them,
my parents, the couch, their lit cigarettes,
flipped over backward onto my brother and me. My husband
thinks that's a funny story and, in an effort to be a "good sport,"
I say I think it is, too.

Which leads me to recall the three Chihuahuas
who've spent the fullness of their agitated lives penned
in the back of my neighbor's yard.
Today they barked continuously for 12 minutes (I timed it) as
the UPS guy made his daily round.
They bark so piercingly, they tremble with such exquisite outrage,
that I've begun to root for them, though it's fashionable
to hate them and increasingly dark threats
against their tiny persons move between the houses on our block.
But isn't that what's wrong with this version of America:
the jittering, small-skulled, inbred-by-no-choice-
of-their-own are despised? And Bill Parcells —
the truth is he'll win

this game. I know it and you know it and, sadly,
did it ever seem there was another possible outcome?

It's a small deposit,
but I'm putting my faith in reincarnation. I need to believe
in the sweetness of one righteous image,
in Bill Parcells trapped in the body of a teacup poodle,
as any despised thing,
forced to yap away his next life staked to
a clothesline pole or doing hard time on a rich old matron's lap,
dyed lilac to match her outfit.
I want to live there someday, across that street,
and listen to him. Yap, yap, yap.

To an Englishman, Lost in Florida

Your grief is an old jazzman sitting with
his legs crossed on a straight-backed chair
and the rain fingering your rented window
is his guitar. He surrounds your room

with the blurred chords of a hurricane refusing
to come. There's nothing to say since the night
you found a giant at your dinner table, foreign
locks on your children's home. Now your accent

begs an explanation and local girls in the pool hall
guess wrongly from where you came: Australia?
Savannah? Try not to speak when you touch them.

You'll abide, knowing the brightest tongues are
made of water, though your boat sits on blocks in
your new roommates' driveway. The bow won't stop
filling with green needles the storm tears loose.

I can't carry the tune soft enough to comfort you,
though I've been to your country, can picture your
boyhood, that postcard of ruins made comfy for
the tourists. They spread their picnics on a pyre, where
Queen Boadicea lit every Roman soul at the wick of
her righteous sorrow. Strangers came to take her

daughters, too. Legend says, plant your shovel in
the earth of Colchester and to this day you'll turn over
a mouth of ash. So the history of rage shakes its long tail
with an embered rattle on the end. My friend,
                                I wish you another music.

In Ecstasy

at the altarpiece of Saint Teresa

No need to be coy—
you know what
she's doing.

And so did Bernini,
when he found Teresa
in the full-throttle of
her divine vision,
        caught her at it,

carving this surrender
so fluidly you expect
the impossible:

for her tang to swell up, ripe
as seafoam, from the gulf
of her flushed and falling
figure. Perhaps this is how

God comes to us,
or should come to us, all:

the bluntly and
beautifully corporeal at

prayers in the Sunday
school of pleasure. Why

shouldn't He come to us
as He did to Teresa? A saint

on her back—
a girl tearing open
the gift He gave her?

The Last of the Gentlemen Heartbreakers

Southern romantic that you always
were, what fallacy recalls you better

than the pathetic one?

If lightning fried a single swampy
pine anywhere south of Cincinnati,

you were gassing up the bagpipe and
drinking to your fallen comrade

before it hit the ground.

You had the knack I admire for self-
satisfaction, a gift for the dubious

backward — your cask of port in every
port and a woman in every storm.

Oh, True Love and Subject of My Late
Juvenilia, there wasn't a ribald

particular I didn't come to know:

the yoga instructress on Valentine's Eve,
the xeroxed erotica files

arranged by body part. Did you think
you were the only mastermind with

a stoned cat purring on your lap, a loyal
death squad on retainer? Count it

a child's Christmas miracle that I let
you live. Sources report you're still

irresistible, a waltz-step elegy
with a showy limp, the same

theme-park pirate in a soiled black
patch, but why insist on covering

your good eye?

You know I don't mean this,
as some girls say, in the *bad* way.

To be fair, you were generous with
a camellia and were born knowing

when to offer a lady your handkerchief.

In the Graveyard

Conceited boy, even here, in the angels' waiting
room, where the dead win all the beauty
contests by default, you arrived with the sun
behind you, working your counterfeit halo,
true as a tin star. It's a fine effect. But today,

for once, you take second to the ugly
jailbreak of azaleas rioting behind us, where
I kiss you again and we linger on the bench
of a long-gone husband's plot. Though,

if you are what I think you are, with terrible
friends in sublime places, explain to me your
cold kind of heart, unmoved by the inappropriate.
Teach me to survive you. Tell me, what kind

won't choose these awful flowers? Who
refuses this bleating, urgent pink?

One for My Baby

colemanite white   livid cicatrix

that scar

left sometime in the '90s   during your black-light

bright   unpromising 20s   acetylene   that night

(whoolordy!)   what didn't happen?   who

knew a lung collapsed so easily?

and the car lighter briefly   kissed your wrist —

not a name   you write in the family

bible   it was   nothing   (trust me)   a fetching

stubble   a season wolfed down to

the ground   clean and ugly the winter

           fields   gray   something   grew there till

may day   and now it's all

                blizzards   blizzards   blizzards

as far as your eye   can't see   but still

                the minuscule moon on the bone

where you've worn it for X

                            many years — so discreet and sure

why wouldn't it hurt   a little?   for instance   people

       leave   like road burns   and abrasions:

remember the girl   on the green line train

           who said   *but grief is for suckers*

mom   to the woman in the seat   beside me   squashing

                     a damp paper bag

to her face   and the girl now   just a voice   a high girlish meanness   how

incongruous   I thought   that veil of

gloss   burying her   kissing her   pretty   (I don't   forget

your fucking)   her   unkind mouth

Below Zero

Every day was a wrong holiday

in your cobalt-colored rooms,

your rented catacombs

laid in with toys and whiskered candy,

a collection of dead men's hats,

dead monkeys and tuxedos, the rot

of expensive cheeses and drugstore

milk fuming in your sink—

where the fan chopped like a guillotine,

where the sheets were always clean,

and where the white fairy appeared nightly

riding Western on De Quincey's

crocodile, crossing her beautiful legs,

batting her wet mosquito wings.

She spoke fluent Irrawaddy. She tickled your

Vandyke. She topped you off for free,

your crystal highball filling like

the well above a pure gin spring.

Who could compete in that marketplace,

that bazaar of happy endings and

endless dunes of blow? If I was the black

diamond of your narcoleptic dreams, then

she was the wish you make for more

wishes, a vicuña-lined pussy

with extra slots for your credit cards.

What mortal could win you? Not I,

my love, no better than any junkie,

the scab fondling your infection,

or worse, the bored lifeguard

jonesing for someone to drown.

Liar's Karma

Assassin, asshole, fine craftsman of myth and malice,
old friend of many years, what was your cause,

Iago? And that afternoon, ear glued to the door, you
spying while he took me hard against the other side,

is that what made you vicious? Did you want him, too?
I'll never know your reasons. But now you live with them,

alone in a peeling bungalow that reeks of the animals who
shit themselves twice daily trying to love you, where a snake

with your mother's face coils like a Freudian cartoon
in the crumbs behind your stove. From the street, I see

you've taken down the curtains in your living room, afraid
of what they're keeping out, but watch how the sunlight bends

around your windows, unwilling to waste itself on dirt
where nothing grows. Consider this your permanent address,

in stunted rooms where fear barely scrapes up the mortgage
and envy ties a hangman's full Windsor around

your neck. Trust me, you'll suffer that silky tongue, friend.
It's the sorrow you made me, the knot frenching your throat.

Pity

Once I took it in my mouth, I had to
admit, pity tastes good, like the sandwiches

they make in French patisseries, the loaf smeared
with force-fed organs, crust that shreds the skin behind

your teeth. So bless the tongue's willingness,

for it chooses like a wartime whore and it's the picky
who end up dead against the wall. And bless also

the bouncers, who all last summer grew kindly
ashamed those nights I fell backward

off their stools. When A. said, "People are generous
with ugly things and you're the Goodwill drop box,"

I counted the turns I've taken on that swing—

the handouts I've offered to the fucked-up
and broken. It's the playground rule,

everyone gets a ride: then you're the girl at the party
trashing the patio furniture, or the man, later

that night, pushing her down in the street.

Shooting Range

Aren't you just like the Daddy every girl dreams of, with your handgun
cocked and your pants pockets full of dirty peppermints? You taught
me to aim at nothing, but a bullet likes to bury itself and we're all
equally worthy — this ridge of drought-colored trees, concrete back-
stop pocked with ammo, redneck in a camo bikini fondling her
boyfriend's Glock — everything thrilled to surrender, asking the same
question we've always had in common: Who's the better killer? You've
had more practice, but I'm a natural. So step a little to the left and I'll
do you the favor. Then you do me. Wasn't that the deal? This day's so
blue, so pretty, let's smash it under glass — a last, weepy moment you'll
remember someday, living in your future, another hit man gone to
wind and belly, selling your glory-holed stories to a new ingenue on
the final installment plan.

iii

Remember me, like a mouth that
opens on the dark. I'll remember you
like a grave forgets what fills it.

JOSH BELL, "SURVIVING LOVE"

In the Red Dress I Wear to Your Funeral

I root through your remains,

looking for the black box. Nothing left

but glossy chunks, a pimp's platinum

tooth clanking inside the urn. I play you

over and over, my beloved conspiracy,

my personal Zapruder film — look,

here's us rounding the corner, here's me

waving at the crowd. God, you were lovely

in your seersucker suit. And weren't we happy

then, before the cross-fire triangulation?

Answer me, dead man.

Wait. Here comes the best part,

where my head snaps back and you crawl

blood-addled and ferocious

from the moving vehicle...

2

I am undead and sulfurous. I stink like a tornado.

I lift my scarlet tail above your grave

and let the idiot villagers take me

in torchlight

one by one by one by one...

Your widowed Messalina, my soprano

cracks the glasses on the buffet at the after party.

I know you can hear me.

Is my hair not coiffed like the monster's bride,

lightning bolts screeching at my temples?

What electrified me

but your good doctor's hand alone?

3

I'm a borscht-belt comedienne

working the audience from behind

your headstone.

I shimmy onstage between Pam

& Her Magic Organ and

the gigantic poodle act.

Your coffin is a tough room.

Mourners talk through my set,

down schmutz-colored highballs, wait

for the fan dancer to pluck

her scuzzy feathers. But you

always loved

the livestock, didn't you?

I say, How many of you folks are in

from Jersey?

The microphone sweats

like your cock did in my hands.

4

I help the Jews drape the mirrors. I peel the foil from

the Protestant's bleak casseroles. The Catholics and Agnostics

huddle in the parking lot, smoking a memorial bowl.

My dear, even the worst despot in his leopard-skin fez

will tell you: the truth doesn't win, but it makes an appearance,

though it's a foreign cavalry famous for bad timing and

half-assed horsemanship. History will barely remember that you

were yellow and a cheat, a pixilated bivalve who consumed

as randomly as the thunderheads pass, and yet, how strange,

how many of us loved you well. So tenderly, I'll return

what you gave me — a bleached handkerchief, a Swiss army knife

bristling with pointless blades. Tenderly, I return everything,

leaving my best evidence in your bloodless lap.

5

I go to our Chinese takeaway,

where the place mats say I'm a snake

and you were my favorite pig, though

astrologically you were a wasting

disease and I'm the scales of justice.

Coincidence?

Get down on your knees

and cross yourself all you want:

all systems are closed systems, dead man.

I keep my saltshaker holstered in my garter belt,

ready to spill.

6

I recite the fairy tale

in which only I can save you: it's our story,

so there's a swamp instead of a forest,

and no trail but a river agog with water moccasins

winding through the cypress knees.

Your faithful Gerda, true sister

in my red pinafore,

I've tracked you doggedly for miles,

appearing at the critical moment,

when you take the Turkish delight into your mouth.

I've arrived just in time!

It's impossible to miss me, eager as a stain

behind the Swamp Queen's white shoulder,

your tattered avenger, your loyal roach, who's wanted only

you in every suppurating hut, who's belly-crawled

through the shit-filled bogs to find you,

to whom you gave your vow, my will undone, family

asunder, my home disappeared by the charm of

your girlish tears...

                     and that's it. Nothing comes next.

That's the moment you decide, dead man.

You look into my face and gulp her

candy down. You shoot it like a bad oyster.

No matter how I tell it, this ends when

you swallow.

7

I was never your Intended,

never meant to be the official widow

like that plain, chinless girl I refused to recognize

or comprehend.

But the plain ones are patient, aren't they?

I'll admit, she's earned her orchestra seats

at this burial the old-fashioned way.

She's up front, next to your mama,

that Chanel commando baked medium-well

in her spray-on tan. A rare example

of a real Southern lady—how many nights

did it cost her, patrolling

the family compound for Jezebels like me?

Your women, dead man. From here

they look like two snap peas squatting

in the same pod.

And they did their job, didn't they?

They made it easy for you?

But later, once the ladies go,

I'll climb down to you again.

I'll come to you in that dirty box

where we've already slept for years,

keeping our silent house

under their avalanche of flowers.

8

EYE AM THE PROMISED VISITATION

PRIESTESS OF BLACK POPLARS

MY TREES R HUNG W/ BRAZEN BELLS

EYE HAVE AUGURED THE PREGNANT SOW'S INTESTINES

RORSCHACHED   THE PICKLED WORM

GLUED TO THE BOTTOM OF YR SHOT GLASS

EYE BRING U NEWS OF   THE UNIVERSE

AND THE NEWS   AINT GOOD   DEAD MAN

B-HOLD!

THE ZOMBIE COCKTAIL HOUR   OF THE YEARS TO CUM

A PURGATORY   UNBENDING AS

A BADLANDS

HI-WAY

IN THE T-LEAVES   EYE SPY YR OUTLINE

YR CORPSE   SNORING IN A VINE-

STRANGLED HOUSE

REBEL DRAG MOUNTS THE WALLS   LIKE A CONFEDERATE

HARD ROCK CAFE   O! THE BLURRED DAYZ

COLLAPSING INTO DINNERS   WHILE THE MAID BURNS

THE FAMILY BISCUITS   & YR WOMAN BEATS

THE GRAVY STIFF   U ARE LOST

GANYMEDE   GONE THAT BOY

WHO POURED HIMSELF   WHOLE INTO THE SIBYL'S

LOVING CUP   NOW EYE CUM

TO BURY U

4 EYE AM

        THE GHOST OF X-MAS PAST   AND YR FUTURE

     BEGINS   NOW   DEAD MAN

9

I do not desist in my delusion   do not permit the victor's

history   will not admit your fake religion   what jams your fingers

in the dry vagina of tin idylls   will not   will not   go

quietly   your evil goody   who cries me in the marketplace   who

knocks my ear to the pillory with false instruments   my crimes

never crimes   for firstly   I be the pretty pony of all plague

slant-gashed   a coil beneath my scum of loveliness   No!   I was

I always am   your yellow roses in a beer bottle   your weakness

and reward   one organ   conjoined in the blue teepee   of floating

whistles   doubled thunder coming   in my wicked mouth   to eat

you and your grandma   too   Name her! Name her   who bites you

harder   little girl!   Will not say   for seconds I am filth   dirty as the damaged apple   I bore   not yours   never yours   that

unspeakable sunshine   Turn your head!   Turn your head   and

I'll kindly cut it off   Yes Yes   the best reason   I am left only

the mother of a great sun   you would go blind and   blinder

to look upon its number and   for finally I am not   of your being

being Queen of the flat kingdoms what crop your emptiness   I do not

admit these   nor I lied   nor I betrayed   nor I am starving   for you

nor can you   make me   never   Will   I disappear

10

I peel myself

and wherever these rubied

feathers drop, a poppy unfurls

in the graveyard, each head plush

as a stitched lip.

            You're right,

it gets me high, how thin I am, my

love, the substance uncontrolled.

But this molting becomes me,

your naturally occurring razor,

your baby IV. Now I am fashioned

the gun so truly fired,

I blast like a magic cap through

my own skin. So go on,

throw the bones

to your hairy pack and let them gnaw.

I'm done with the meat. Soon, I'll be

demolished. I'll step away free.

iv

At Last

In this story
   no one dies

and no one's left living
   in a cardboard box.

And the laughing owls
   that squat in the trees above
      your neighborhood

   still cackle to themselves nightly,
      a synchronized posse
         of madwomen

committed to the skeletal pines.

   In the end, what you loved moves
      to Brooklyn. That's all.

         And if there's recompense,

      it comes to you, impartial as
         the nanny's hand into

her charge's honeycomb of fever.
     It comes to remind you

         that even the millionth tragedy
            went uncelebrated the day

the world was born. No cake.
     No sacred confetti —

     it just toddled away
         to roll down someone else's hill.

Consider all the paintings gathered
     in the world's great museums —

         what collects there
            but the manuals of chaos,

frescoes of bad faith displayed
     between a few innocuous

         landscapes? —

the outraged sisters of Lucrece
     bleeding and wailing or

         John the Baptist, served up on silver —

always the same betrayals dressed
       in period costume.

    But the day comes,
        with or without you, when

the tea olive waving its arms
       over the back fence puts up

its white-flowered fuss again, arguing
       for sweetness.

About the Author

Erin Belieu is the author of two previous poetry collections from Copper Canyon Press — *Infanta,* which was chosen for the National Poetry Series in 1995, and *One Above & One Below,* which won the Midland Authors and Ohioana prizes in 2001. Belieu is also the co-editor (with Susan Aizenberg) of the anthology *The Extraordinary Tide: New Poetry by American Women* (Columbia University Press, 2001). Her poems have appeared in places such as *The Atlantic Monthly, The Best American Poetry, The New York Times, Ploughshares, Slate, Tin House, TriQuarterly,* and *The Virginia Quarterly Review.* Born and raised in the great state of Nebraska, Belieu studied poetry at The Ohio State University and Boston University. She now lives in Tallahassee, Florida, and teaches in the Creative Writing Program at Florida State University.

The Chinese character for poetry is made up of two parts: "word" and "temple." It also serves as pressmark for Copper Canyon Press. Founded in 1972, Copper Canyon Press remains dedicated to publishing poetry exclusively, from Nobel laureates to new and emerging authors. The Press thrives with the generous patronage of readers, writers, booksellers, librarians, teachers, students, and funders—everyone who shares the conviction that poetry invigorates the language and sharpens our appreciation of the world.

Major funding has been provided by:

Anonymous (2)

The Paul G. Allen Family Foundation

Lannan Foundation

National Endowment for the Arts

Washington State Arts Commission

THE **PAUL G. ALLEN** **FAMILY** *foundation*

Lannan

N A T I O N A L
E N D O W M E N T
FOR THE ARTS

For information and catalogs:

COPPER CANYON PRESS
Post Office Box 271
Port Townsend, Washington 98368
360-385-4925
www.coppercanyonpress.org

■

This book is set in FF Acanthus Text, designed by Akira Kobayashi after a type specimen from 1788 by Henri Didot. The titles are set in Cochin and Cochin Bold. Georges Peignot designed Cochin based on eighteenth-century engravings and Charles Malin cut the typeface in 1912 for Deberny & Peignot. Interior design and composition by Valerie Brewter, Scribe Typography. Printed on archival-quality Glatfelter Author's Text by McNaughton & Gunn.